The ABCs of Derpetology

Jessica Lee Anderson

AO PRESS

Paperback ISBN: 978-1-964078-08-3

To Micha Petty, thanks for creating Derpetology to foster reptile positivity and for advancing education and rescuing/rehabbing so many critters! -JLA

Micha Petty holds many titles including author, licensed wildlife rehabilitator, and Louisiana Master Naturalist. Micha was inspired to begin a popular online group called Derpetology after creating this meme on the right. Derpetology is derived from the word herpetology (the study of reptiles and amphibians), and it is a celebration of derpy herps of all kinds. This book is an homage to Derpetology and L.E.A.R.N. (Louisiana Exotic Animal Resource Network), the reptile rescue center at the heart of it all. Derp enthusiasts (reptile keepers, animal rehabilitators, wildlife photographers, and more) contributed every picture in this book. Thank you to everyone for sharing and for being part of this project to help raise funds for L.E.A.R.N.

SNAKES ON TV BE LIKE

SNAKES I ACTUALLY FIND

White-lipped Pitviper photo by Tontan Travel CC BY 2.0
Plain-bellied Watersnake photo by David Busch

@LiveSnakes

This Book Belongs to:

_____

A is for Athletic

Yellow-Bellied Slider

Soren Lorenson - Leopard Gecko

Casque-Headed Iguana

Garlic - Gargoyle Gecko

Nuggie - Ackie Monitor

Denali - Crested Gecko

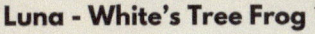

Luna - White's Tree Frog

Sam - Crested Gecko

Caiman Lizard

Derpy Detail

Many kinds of reptiles and amphibians have adaptations such as grippy feet or webbing that make them atheltic superstars.

A a

Simon & Garfunkel - Veiled Chameleons

 B is for Babies

Ari - Buckskin Okeetee Corn Snake

Ackie Monitors

Udon - Anery Kenyan Sand Boa

Bartholomew - Aldabra Tortoise

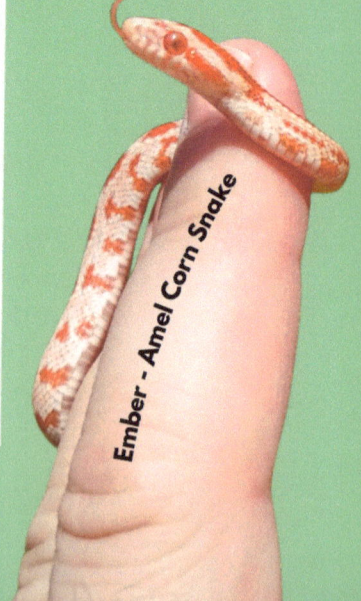
Ember - Amel Corn Snake

Derpy Detail

Certain reptiles lay eggs while others give live birth. Most amphibians lay jellylike eggs near water (or even under rocks or logs), though a few give live birth.

Common Snapping Turtle

Ember - Amel Corn Snake Hatchling

Arthur - Western Hognose

Kemp's Ridley Sea Turtle

Central Bearded Dragon

Lilah - Super Fire Ball Python

B b

C is for Cozy

Hot Dog Princess - Mueller's Sand Boa

Sproggle - Blue-Tongued Skink

Sissler - Red Corn Snake

Lumi - Cinnamon Champagne Ball Python

Bubonic - Amel Corn Snake

Baguette - Northern Blue-Tongued Skink

Tiny Tina - BCI/BCC Hybrid Boa

Sir Ratsford Hissington - Black Ratsnake

Rigatoni - Genetic Stripe Ball Python

Jormi - Western Hognose

C c

is for Dashing

Rog - Pacman Frog

Black Mamba

Yveltal- Tomato Frog

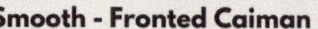

Smooth - Fronted Caiman

Pickett - Leopard Gecko

Unisexual Ambystoma Complex

Sgaeyl - Blue-Spotted Tree Monitor

Mountain Earth Snake

Derpy Detail

Reptiles have scales on their skin that can vary in size and shape. Amphibians don't have scales.

Chico - Smooth-Fronted Caiman

Ruth - Crested Gecko

Curious George - Buckskin Okeetee Corn Snake

D d

 **is for Expressive Eyes**

Poocasso - Leachianus Gecko

Queso - Trans-Pecos Ratsnake

Rune - Brindle Inkspot Dalmation Crested Gecko

Garlic - Gargoyle Gecko

Pyro - Axolotl

Opal - White's Tree Frog

Hoggle - Western Hognose

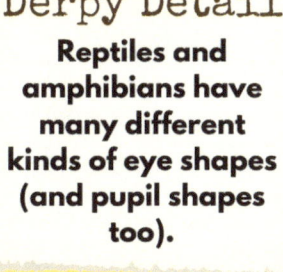

Hazel - Eastern Gartersnake

Tiger Salamander

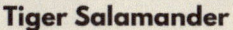

Vietnamese Black-Breasted Leaf Turtle

Eastern Hognose

E e

is for Freckly

Gulf Coast Toad

George - Leopard Gecko

Sprout - Yellow Dalmation Crested Gecko

Eastern Spadefoot

Harley Quinn - Palmetto Corn Snake

Tibby - Hog Island Boa

14

Couch's Spadefoot Toad

Cave Salamander

Spotted Salamander

Burrowing Toad

Derpy Detail

Certain reptiles and amphibians have spots and bumps which helps them blend into their environment. Camouflage protects animals from predators.

Yucatan Banded Gecko

Sir Hopper Hoppington the 3rd - Eastern Toad

F f

is for Glamorous

Taika - Central Bearded Dragon

Lucifer - Western Hognose

Derpy Detail
Researchers are studying how reptiles and amphibians use chemical signals to communicate.

Harry - Margin Red Base Crested Gecko

Nitro - Red-Footed Tortoise

16

Fizzgig - Central Bearded Dragon

Gotham - Western Hognose

Lyle - Morelet's Crocodile

Boogie - African Bullfrog

Fika - Central Bearded Dragon

G g

is for Hats

Gulpin - Pacman Frog

Splash thee Turtle - Red-Eared/Yellow-Bellied Slider Hybrid

Atreus - Savannah Monitor

Rad - Bredl's Python

Noodle - Western Hognose

Captain Blackbeard - Central Bearded Dragon

Ripley - Blue-Tongued Skink

Chaos - Eastern Indigo

Boogie - African Bullfrog

Derpy Detail

Certain reptile and amphibian species have a "third eye" on the top of their heads—a pineal gland that senses light.

H h

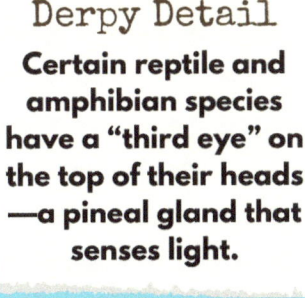

Colby Jack - Gargoyle Gecko

19

I is for Imperial

Garmadon - Red Leatherback Central Bearded Dragon

Tanimbar Python

Sylvie - Three-Toed Box Turtle

King Leon - Cream Crested Gecko

Ivan - Western Hognose

20

Dug - Irian Jaya Blue-Tongued Skink

Eastern Hognose

Fizzgig - Central Bearded Dragon

Dirk - Central Bearded Dragon

Eastern Box Turtle

l i

Oracle - Tripod Tegu

21

is for Judgy

Eastern Box Turtle

Jose - Crested Gecko

Mustard & Dijon - Moroccan Uromastyx

Whale - Mottled Rock Rattlesnake

Galápagos Giant Tortoise

Yucatan Casque-Headed Treefrog

Tonks - Eastern Hermanns Tortoise

Ripley - Blue-Tongued Skink

Rough Greensnake

Uromastyx

American Bullfrog

Derpy Detail
Herpetologists are continuing to make discoveries about the behaviors of reptiles and amphibians.

Jj

23

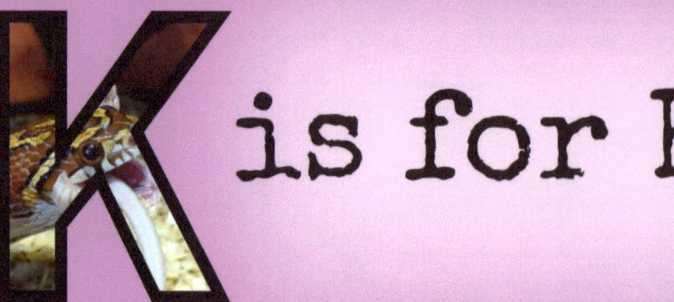 is for Keen

Ball Python

Peep - Kenyan Sand Boa

Ziti - Kenyan Sand Boa

Ms. Greenbean - Veiled Chameleon

Dirk - Central Bearded Dragon

Chewy - Buckskin Okeetee Corn Snake

Oracle - Tripod Tegu

Riker - Blue-Tongued Skink

Kukulkan - Yucatan Rattlesnake

K k

L is for Loopy

Adrian - Pastel Banana Ball Python

Boo - Snow Corn Snake

Derpy Detail

A zoologist named Dr. Roth conducted studies and determined certain snakes prefer to coil in the clockwise direction.

Asmodeus - Reserve Stripe California Striped Kingsnake

Albino Anaconda Western Hognose

Mr. Toad - Western Hognose

Gopher Snake

Lilith - Peppermint Morph Corn Snake

Captain - Red Corn Snake

Pickles - Green Tree Python

Noodle - Western Hognose

L l

27

 is for Mouthy

Charlie - Black Roughneck Monitor

Billy - Pacman Frog

Eastern Hognose

American Alligator

Grover - Australian Green Treefrog

Derpy Detail
Some reptiles such as crocodilians (alligators, crocodiles, caiman, etc.) will gape with their mouths open while basking to regulate temperature (kind of like a dog panting).

Galápagos Giant Tortoise

Jiminy Cricket - Crested Gecko

South American Bushmaster

Sobek - Tokay Gecko

Eastern Collared Lizard

Clint - Frilled Lizard

Majora - Red-Lipped Arboreal Alligator Lizard

M m

is for Nosy

Beast - Het Anery Argentine Tegu

Nuggie - Ackie Monitor

Eastern Box Turtle

Derpy Detail

Reptiles and amphibians have nostrils that allow them to breathe oxygen. Amphibians can also breathe through their skin.

Krooky - Gila Monster

Leeloo - Tessera Corn Snake

Cave Salamander

**Splash thee Turtle -
Red-Eared/Yellow-Bellied Slider Hybrid**

Zilla - Argentine Tegu

**Jupiter - Asian Water
Monitor**

Vincent -Blood Python

Green Bean - Rhinoceros Ratsnake

N n

is for Ornate

Bog Turtle

Rango - Crested Gecko

Frilled Lizard

Eastern Box Turtle

Ms. Greenbean - Veiled Chameleon

Meller's Chameleon

Kane (kah-nay) - Red Niger Uromastyx

Green Sea Turtle

Burrowing Toad

Four-Horned Chameleon

Derpy Detail

Reptiles and amphibians vary in markings, patterns, and colors. Some are even adorned with interesting accessories!

is for Periscope

Mickey Mouse - Anery Motley Corn Snake

Ari - Buckskin Okeetee Corn Snake

Jormi - Western Hognose

Derpy Detail
Some kinds of snakes use their neck and trunk muscles to periscope so they can check out areas around them.

Western Green Mamba

Rigatoni - Ball Python

34

Blunt-Headed Treesnake

Whale - Mottled Rock Rattlesnake

Jake - Anery Corn Snake

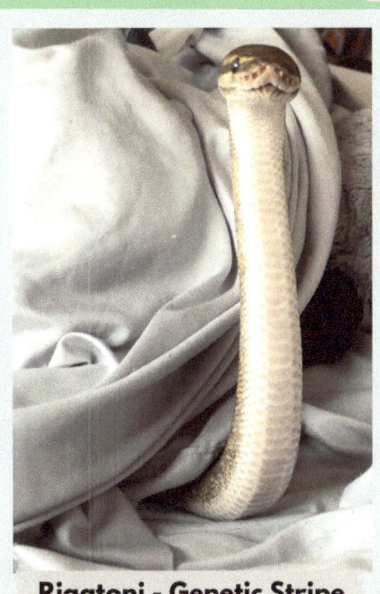

Rigatoni - Genetic Stripe Ball Python

Master Splinter - Banana YB Ball Python

P p

Q is for Quizzical

Cupcake - Children's Python

Annie - Schneider's Skink

Texas Spiny Lizard

Mango - Crested Gecko

Mabel - Central Bearded Dragon

Sir Ratsford Hissington - Black Ratsnake

Pyro - Axolotl

Pumpernickel - Western Hognose

Dug - Irian Jaya Blue-Tongued Skink

Derpy Detail

Most reptiles and amphibians have voluntary control of their pupils (meaning they can constrict or dilate in response to light when they want to).

Q q

Dirk - Central Bearded Dragon

R is for Relaxed

Three-Toed Box Turtle

Gharial

Baguette - Northern Blue-Tongued Skink

Rocky - Central Bearded Dragon

Reptiles and amphibians need their beauty rest too!

Green Tree Monitor

Ozzy - Central Bearded Dragon

Common Snapping Turtle

Northern False Map Turtle

Zilla - Argentine Tegu

R r

S is for Silly Sheds

Garlic - Gargoyle Gecko

General Eon - Green Anole

Sissler - Red Corn Snake

Derpy Detail

Amphibians and reptiles shed their skin regularly throughout their lives (and some eat their shed skin for nutrients).

Buddy - Buckskin Okeetee Corn Snake

Eastern Copperhead

George - Leopard Gecko

Cupcake - Children's Python

Northern Ring-Necked Snake

S s

Riot - Crested Gecko

T is for Tongue Out

Nagini - Western Hognose

Kratos - Asian Water Monitor

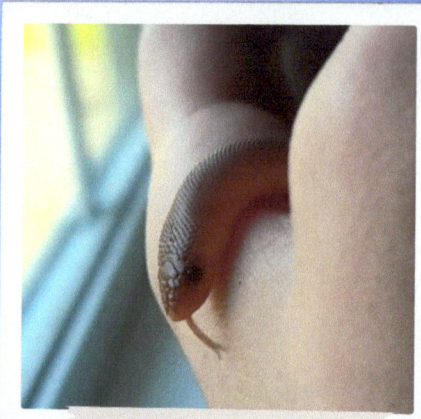
De Selby - Rubber Boa

Blitz - Central Bearded Dragon

Charlie - Black Roughneck Monitor

Newt - Crested Gecko

Komodo Dragon

Kukulkan - Yucatan Rattlesnake

Apopis - T-Albino African House Snake

Alucard - Blood Python

Derpy Detail

Several reptile and amphibian species have strong and sticky tongues (like some chameleons and frogs). Some reptiles like snakes use their tongues to smell the air!

T t

Boba - Ball Python

43

is for Upside Down

Fika - Central Bearded Dragon

Ziggy - Cream Pinstripe Crested Gecko

Havarti - Kuhl's Flying Gecko

Doctor Who - Kuhl's Flying Gecko

44

Snape - Western Hognose

Majora - Red-Lipped Arboreal Alligator Lizard

Setaro's Dwarf Chameleon

River Song- Kuhl's Flying Gecko

Derpy Detail

Certain reptiles can live up in the air thanks to adaptations like belly scales, sharp nails, prehensile tails, and special toe pads.

U u

V is for Vibrant

Yellow-Eyed Ensatina

Costa Rican Dart Frog

Athena - Mexican Black Kingsnake

Cope's Gray Treefrog

Yucatan Casque-Headed Treefrog

46

**Rune - Brindle Inkspot
Dalmation Crested Gecko**

**Boba Fett - Ambilobe
Panther Chameleon**

Sage - Dart Frog

Magnificent Treefrog

Pickles - Green Tree Python

Chaos - Eastern Indigo

V v

W is for Wild

Diamondback Watersnake

Northern Cottonmouth

Common Five-Lined Skink

Eastern Copperhead

Barking Treefrog

Common Snapping Turtle

Northern Watersnake

Western Ratsnake

American Bullfrog

Eastern Gartersnake

Eastern Red-Backed Salamander

Derpy Detail

Amphibians and reptiles live in a variety of environments like deserts, mountains, wetlands, and rainforests. They are found on every continent except for Antartica.

W w

X  is for Xenial

Burrowing Toads

Hopper & Chrissy - Rankins Dragons

Riot & Red - Crested Geckos

American Alligators

Baguette - Northern Blue-Tongued Skink

Grover and Gretchen - Australian Green Treefrogs

Alexander the Tort, Nefertorti, & King Tort - Sulcata Tortoises

Sobek (Cuvier's Dwarf Caiman) & Franklin (Musk Turtle)

Hourglass Treefrogs

Rigatoni (Ball Python) & Ziti (Kenyan Sand Boa)

Derpy Detail

Certain reptiles and amphibians exhibit xenial behaviors (hospitable and tolerant of others).

X x

51

Y is for Yawn

Valen - Bongo Ghi Banana Ball Python

Jake - Anery Corn Snake

Smooth Greensnake

Chaos - Eastern Indigo

Derpy Detail

Snakes appear to yawn before or after a meal as they stretch or realign their jaws. In some species, an open mouth is a warning sign to potential threats.

Cornflake - Buckskin Corn Snake

Eastern Hognose

Inosuke - Pinstripe Ball Python

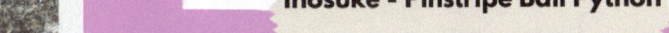

Eastern Cottonmouth
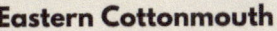

Gotham - Western Hognose

Cayenne - Reticulated Python

Y y

 Z is for Zoning Out

Duckie - Super Dwarf Reticulated Python

Twig - Crested Gecko

Leachianus Gecko

Rune - Brindle Inkspot Dalmation Crested Gecko

Mexican Treefrog

Blanding's Turtle

Crested Gecko

Sheep Frog

Giant Monkey Frog

Z z

Derpy Detail

Most species of reptiles and amphibians have four kinds of color receptors—their ability to see color beats the color perception of cats and dogs!

Thanks to all of the contributors for making this book possible!

Photo credits—Front Cover: Nadine Schriver (Lennard - Leopard Gecko); Back Cover: Bob Ferguson (Large-Blotched Ensatina); Cover Page: Jayden Pettigrew; Copyright Page: Micha Petty; Dedication Page (top to bottom, left to right): Carrie E. Moyers, Sam Reynolds, Wendy Horton, Emilys_Critters, Boogie's Mom Stephanie, Craig Randall, Bob Ferguson, Jennifer Wolber - Heretic Reptiles; p. 4: A: Jacqueline E. Smith (Green Anole), Jennifer Tuttle, Christy Robertson, Bob Ferguson, Rachel Charles, Kyle's Monitors; p. 5: C. Robinson (Luna and Sam), Leanore Morgan, Craig Randall, Rayechelly Berrelez; p. 6: B: Craig Randall, Ava Anderson, Kyle's Monitors, Courtney, Rory L. Harris & Mai Lee Vang, Craig Randall; p. 7: Carrie E. Moyers, Craig Randall, Sage Thompson, Jacqueline E. Smith, Craig Randall, Alexxa Standifer; p. 8: C: Christy Robertson, Alex Kawano, Emily Harkness, Myles Weck, Thrystan Wouters, Brittany 'Rat' Frazier; p. 9: Nicole Pratt, White Lotus Serpents, Matthew Parks, Grace Fiacco, Krystal Braza; p. 10: D: Christy Robertson (Hazel - Rankins Dragon), Christy Robertson, Bob Ferguson, Taylor Tansey, Jeremy & Janelle Humphrey/Ace's Reptile Emporium, Leanore Morgan; p. 11: Freya the Wolf, Alexis Weckwerth, Bob Ferguson, Owner of House of Exotics, Emilys_Critters, Craig Randall; p. 12: E: Evelyn Ashdown - Spitfire Hogs, Mackenzie Winters, Taylor Tansey, Hailey Stephenson, Rachel Charles, Francesca DiGeronimo; p. 13: Myles Weck, Wendy Horton, Jacqueline E. Smith, Katie Wenstrom, Bob Ferguson (salamander and hognose); p. 14: F: Jeremy & Janelle Humphrey/Ace's Reptile Emporium (Madagascan Giant Hognose), Whovian Geckos, Craig Randall (toad, gecko, snake), Bob Ferguson, A. Johnson; p. 15: Craig Randall, Bob Ferguson, Jennifer Tuttle, Freya the Wolf, Bob Ferguson, Jesse Durham; p. 16: Evelyn Ashdown - Spitfire Hogs, Christy Robertson, Whovian Geckos, Taylor Tansey; p. 17: Stephanie Pilisko, Evelyn Ashdown - Spitfire Hogs, Drippin Dragons, Boogie's Mom Stephanie, Jennifer Raichman; p. 18: H: Emilys_Critters (Blue-Tongued Skink), Emilys_Critters, Splash_thee_Turtle, Antonia van Koeverden, Emily Harkness, B. Crist; p. 19: Jessica Lee Anderson, Emilys_Critters, Kyrsten with Hudson Valley Reptile & Rescue, Boogie's Mom Stephanie, Alexis Weckwerth; p. 20: I: Jacqueline E. Smith (Green Anole), Drippin Dragons, T. H. Wyman, Carrie E. Moyers, C. Robinson, Jessica Mailloux; p. 21: Justin Jewell, Bob Ferguson, Stephanie Pilisko, Jimmy G., Jennifer Tuttle, Jennyfer Keohane; p. 22: J: C. Robinson (Hermann's Tortoise), Carrie E. Moyers, Toni Smith, The Young Family Herpetoculture Collective, Rory L. Harris & Mai Lee Vang, Jacqueline E. Smith, p. 23: Bob Ferguson, C. Robinson, Emilys_Critters, Bob Ferguson, Craig Randall, Jacqueline E. Smith; p. 24: K: Craig Randall (Corn Snake), Amanda S., Stephanie Pilisko, Grace Fiacco, The Children of SitH; p. 25: Jimmy G., Craig Randall, Jennyfer Keohane, Rory L. Harris & Mai Lee Vang, Emilys_Critters; p. 26: L: Alexxa Standifer (Ball Python), Carrie E. Moyers, C. Robinson, Whovian Geckos, Jeremy & Janelle Humphrey/Ace's Reptile Emporium; p. 27: Manda Cradit, Bob Ferguson, Jennifer Wolber - Heretic Reptiles, Jordan Jackson, Sam Reynolds, B. Crist; p. 28: M: Emilys_Critters (Neon Day Gecko), Katie Wenstrom, Myles Weck, Bob Ferguson, Jacqueline E. Smith, Emily Carreiro; p. 29: Jacqueline E. Smith, Manda Cradit, Bob Ferguson, Whovian Geckos, Bob Ferguson, M. Baelemans, Savannah Noland, (Perfect Hue LLC); p. 30: N: C. Robinson (Fred - Corn Snake),

Photo credits cont'd—R & R Dragons, Kyle's Monitors, Bob Ferguson, Taylor Tansey, Stephanie Pilisko; p. 31: Arwyn Tuttle, Splash_thee_Turtle, Wendy Horton, Owner of House of Exotics, Sarah Gaynor (Bluebonnet Bloods), Katie Hundley; p. 32: Jennifer Tuttle (Eastern Box Turtle), Bob Ferguson, Megan N. Davis, Jeremy & Janelle Humphrey/Ace's Reptile Emporium, Carrie E. Moyers, The Children of SitH; p.33: Craig Randall, The Young Family Herpetoculture Collective, Bob Ferguson (sea turtle and toad), Jacqueline E. Smith; p. 34: P: Stephanie Pilisko (Corn Snake), Manda Cradit, Ava Anderson, Krystal Braza, Jacqueline E. Smith, Grace Fiacco; p. 35: Bob Ferguson, Rory L. Harris & Mai Lee Vang, Tessa Ray Daniel, Grace Fiacco, Manda Cradit; p. 36: Q: Jacqueline E. Smith (Green Anole), M. Baelemans, Alex Kawano, Jacqueline E. Smith, Rachel Charles, Kristen Yates and Mabel; p. 37: Matthew Parks, Francesca DiGeronimo, Evelyn Ashdown - Spitfire Hogs, Justin Jewell, Jimmy G.; p. 38: R: A. Johnson (Hog Island Boa), Carrie E. Moyers, Jacqueline E. Smith, Nicole Pratt, Emily Carreiro; p. 39: Carrie E. Moyers, Kyle's Monitors, Toni Smith, Jennifer Tuttle, Wendy Horton; 40: S: Craig Randall (Leopard Gecko), Rachel Charles, Thrystan Wouters, Craig Randall (General Eon and Buddy), Bob Ferguson; p. 41: Craig Randall, Jessica Lee Anderson, Bob Ferguson, M. Baelemans, Emilys_Critters; p. 42: T: A. Johnson (Fidget - Lipstick Boa), Evelyn Ashdown - Spitfire Hogs, Antonia van Koeverden, ZOE VON HOLTEN, Drippin Dragons, Katie Wenstrom, Alexandra JD; p. 43: Jacqueline E. Smith, Rory L. Harris & & Mai Lee Vang, Sarah Gaynor (Bluebonnet Bloods), Whovian Geckos, Courtney; p. 44: U: Matthew Parks (black ratsnake), Jennifer Raichman, Makayla Grace Tavares, Alexis Weckwerth, Whovian Geckos; p. 45: Whovian Geckos, Savannah Noland (Perfect Hue LLC), Bob Ferguson, Whovian Geckos; p. 46: V: Jacqueline E. Smith (Rough Reen Snake), Bob Ferguson, Stephanie Pilisko, Jennifer Wolber - Heretic Reptiles, Micha Petty, Bob Ferguson; p. 47: Hailey Stephenson, Brandon Scholl, Sage Thompson, Jacqueline E. Smith, Sam Reynolds, Kyrsten with Hudson Valley Reptile & Rescue; p. 48: W: Jacqueline E. Smith ("Southern" Prairie Skink), Craig Randall, Jennifer Tuttle, Bob Ferguson (Copperhead and Treefrog); p.49: Jennifer Tuttle, Erin Wright, Micha Petty, Jacqueline E. Smith, Freya the Wolf, Jennifer Tuttle; p. 50: X: Grace Fiacco, Drippin Dragons, Bob Ferguson, Emilys_Critters, Jacqueline E. Smith, Nicole Pratt; p. 51: Emily Carreiro, Zach Hoover, Antonia van Koeverden, Antonia van Koeverden, Grace Fiacco; p. 52: Y: Jeremy & Janelle Humphrey/Ace's Reptile Emporium (Crested Gecko), Bruce M. Tavares, Tessa Ray Daniel, Bob Ferguson, Kyrsten - Hudson Valley Reptile & Rescue, Craig Randall; p. 53: Bob Ferguson (Hognose and Cottonmouth), Tessa Ray Daniel, Evelyn Ashdown - Spitfire Hogs, Brittany 'Rat' Frazier; p. 54: Z: Brittany 'Rat' Frazier (Reticulated Python), Alex Kawano, Christy Robertson, Jeremy & Janelle Humphrey/Ace's Reptile Emporium, Hailey Stephenson; p. 55: Bob Ferguson (frogs and turtle), Jeremy & Janelle Humphrey/Ace's Reptile Emporium (Crested Gecko); p. 56: C. Robinson (Western Hognose), Jennifer Wolber - Heretic Reptiles (Mexican Kingsnake), Jacqueline E. Smith (Magnificent Treefrog), Hailey Stephenson (Crested Gecko); 57: Katie Hundley (Rhinoceros Ratsnake), Craig Randall (Amel Corn Snake), ZOE VON HOLTEN (Rubber Boa), Tessa Daniel (Blue-Tongued Skink), Bob Ferguson (Eastern Box Turtle), p. 58: Michael Anderson

Jessica Lee Anderson is an award-winning author of over 75 books for young readers. She writes reptile-positive stories including the NAOMI NASH chapter book series. Jessica lives near Austin, Texas with her daughter, Ava, and husband, Michael. They have a corn snake named Ari they watched hatch from an egg. If a Western Ratsnake visits their yard, you can guarantee there will be a photo op. You can learn more about Jessica by visiting www.jessicaleeanderson.com.

Looking for more ABC books? Check out these titles:

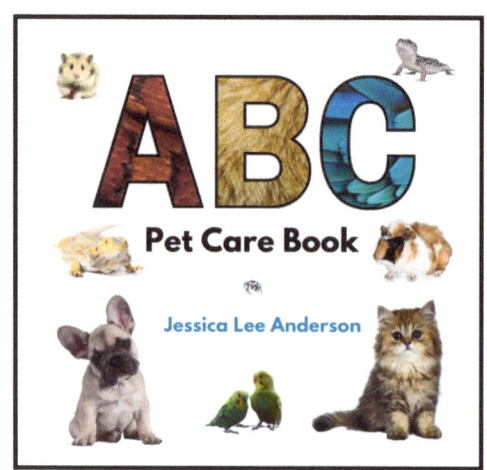

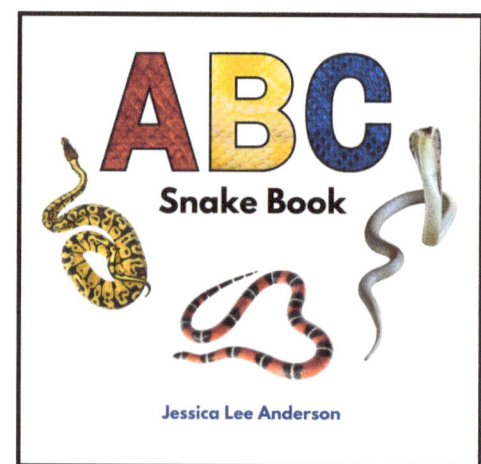

www.ingramcontent.com/pod-product-compliance
Lightning Source LLC
Chambersburg PA
CBHW041553120626
46551CB00002B/190